BEING BILINGUAL

BEING BILINGUAL

A guide for parents, teachers and young people on mother tongue, heritage language and bilingual education

Safder Alladina

tb

Trentham Books

First published in 1995 by Trentham Books Limited

Trentham Books Limited
Westview House
734 London Road
Oakhill
Stoke-on-Trent
Staffordshire
England ST4 5NP

British Cataloguing in Publication Data
A catalogue record for this book is available from the British Library
ISBN: 1 85856 051 9

Designed and typeset by Trentham Print Design Limited, Chester
and printed in Great Britain by Bemrose Shafron (Printers) Limited, Chester

To my mother and father who taught me the first words of my language and who made sure that I continued to develop my Gujerati while I was learning English and other languages.

The cover of this book shows the lotus flower from different cultures. The design was inspired by an article by Dr. D.P. Pattanayak who wrote about the *Monolingual Myopia and the Petals of the Indian Lotus.* Dr. Pattanayak's article is discussed in the second part of this book. The Japanese calligraphy and the black ink drawing — *sumie* — are by Hiro Ajiki. The Urdu calligraphy of the *nilopher* is by Nusrat Jan.

Acknowledgements:

Schoolchildren in London and Vancouver for their drawings; Longman Publishers for the proverbs on languages; United Media for the *Peanuts* cartoon and Angus McGill and Dominic Poelsma for the *Augusta* cartoon.

Contents

FOREWORD

What does it mean to be bilingual? What are the advantages of growing up with two or more languages? Does bilingualism help or hinder the mental and educational development of children? How can children be helped in their language development?

This book has been written for parents, young people and students who would like to discuss these questions and understand more about bilingualism and being bilingual.

In the last twenty years a large number of books and research reports have been written on the subject of mental and educational development of children growing up using more than one language. In most cases, these books are written for scholars and researchers. The result is that parents and young people are faced with a huge amount of reading. If they are not in the business of doing academic reading and research, it is not easy to form an informed opinion. Also, many ideas about language have come down through hearsay and tradition. Although there is wisdom in some of these ideas, there are also ideas that do not give correct information and some of these ideas do not match what scientific research in the last twenty years has revealed about language, thought and the human brain.

This book presents the arguments and research findings simply and straightforwardly so that parents and young people who are interested in the subject can take part in the discussion. I would recommend that parents also involve children, however young, in reading parts of this book. The pictures have been put there to make it interesting to young children. The last section of the book gives summaries of some important research findings and further reading for those who would like to look deeper into the subject.

It is my sincere hope that this book will help to clear the confusion so that we can give our children a language experience that is best for them.

Safder Alladina
Vancouver
1995

WISE WORDS FROM AROUND THE WORLD

اطلب العلم من المهد إلى اللحد

Seek knowledge from the cradle to the grave
(Arabic from the Koran)

El silencio nos ha sido dado para expresar mejor nuestro proprio pensamiento
Silence is given for better hearing our thoughts
(Spanish proverb)

Is buaine port na glor na n-ean
Is buaine focal na toice an tsaoil
A tune is more enduring than the song of the birds
A word is more enduring than the wealth of the world
(Irish proverb)

ਬੋਲੀ ਹੈ ਪੰਜਾਬੀ ਸਾਡੀ।
ਰੂਹ ਜਿੰਦ ਜਾਨ ਸਾਡੀ, ਗਿੱਧਿਆਂ ਦੀ ਖਾਨ ਸਾਡੀ।

Our language is Panjabi. It is our life and soul.
It is a treasure of folk songs.
(Panjabi poem - Chatrik)

Magana jari ce
Speech is wealth
(Hausa proverb)

নানান দেশে   নানান ভাষা
বিনা স্বদেশী ভাষা
মিটেকি আশা।

One can use the languages of other countries, but one can only get fulfilment in the mother tongue
(Bengali poem - Ghupta)

Varesave foki nai-len pengi nogi chib, si kokora posh foki
A people without their own language is only half a people
(British Romani saying)

Kas savo kalbaa niekina - Kitos neismoks
Anyone who devalues their own language will not learn anyone else's
(Lithuanian proverb)

Ang hindi marunong magmahal sa sariling wika, ay masahol pa sa malangsang isda.
Anyone who does not love their own native language is digustingly worse than a smelly fish.
(Tagalog - Jose Rizal)

භාෂාව ජාතියේ රුධිරයයි

Language is the lifeblood of a people
(Sinhala proverb)

Parla comma t'ha fatto mammate
Speak like your mother made you
(Italian proverb - Naples dialect)

Soz Gummusse sukut altindir
If words are silver, silence is golden
(Turkish proverb)

निज भाषा उन्नति अहै,
सब उन्नति कर मूल ।
बिनु निज भाषा ज्ञान के,
मिटत न हिय के सूल ॥

One's language is the provenance
Of all developed thought;
Until we know our mother tongue
Our hearts remain distraught.
(Hindi poem - Harishchandra)

I am neither Christian, nor Jew, nor Zoroastrian nor Moslem
I am not of East nor West; land or sea
I have put duality away, I have seen that the two worlds are one.
One I seek, one I know, one, I see, one I Call
(Farsi (Persian) poem - Rumi)

одне становить нашу народню силу, нашу народню славу, одне дає нам право на дільницю між іншими народами.

The Ukrainian language alone is the strength of our people, he glory of our people, and it alone allows us to claim a place among other nations
(Ukrainian by Kulish)

Heb iaith, heb genedl
No language, no nation
(Welsh proverb)

ix

கற்க கசடறக் கற்பவை கற்றபி
னீற்க வதற்குத் தக.

Learn and learn thoroughly; having learned, live
according to the learning
(Tamil - Thirrukural)

જ્યાં જ્યાં વસે એક ગુજરાતી ત્યાં ત્યાં સદાકાળ ગુજરાત

Wherever a single Gujerati resides, Gujarat is ever there
(Gujarati poem - Khabardar)

*Kau neva no di yus of im*tel *til di butcha kot it of*
The cow didn't know what use her tail was until
the butcher cut it off
(Proverb - Jamaican Creole)

Do Mlodziezy Polskiej.
Ucz sie ojcow twych jezyka
On mysl kazdu
Gnie sie dzwieczy, grzmi, przenika,
jazny, smialy, bo jest wolny.

To the young Polish.
learn your father's mother tongue
It is able to express every thought,
It is flexible, it sounds, thunders, penetrates.
Bright, courageous as it's free
(Polish poem - Kaminski)

یہ اُردو زبان کامل و پُر اثر
زبانوں کی سورج، ادب کی قمر
فصاحت میں پایہ ہے اِس کا بلند
سراپا بلاغت، ذہن پُر گہر

Urdu is an accomplished and forceful language
It is like the sun among the languages and the
moon (of the world) of literature.
It has a great potential for eloquence.
It is full of rhetoric and has pearl-like beauty.
(Urdu - Hamdani)

Parla cuma ta maet
Speak like you eat
(Italian proverb -
Bergamo dialect)

Mot kho vang khong mot nan chu
A house full of gold is not worth a
small bag of learning
(Vietnamese proverb)

A minha patria e a lingua portuguesa
My motherland is the Portuguese language
(Portuguese - Pessoa)

Kweyol-la se yon bel kado
The Kweyol language is a wonderful gift
(Proverb, Creole of St. Lucia)

BEING BILINGUAL

In the last fifty years, large numbers of people have moved from one part of the world to another. Today, the cities of the world are places where many languages are spoken. This is not the first time in the history of the world that this has happened. There have always been cities, towns and countries where many languages have lived together. But in today's world it has become more and more common. The cities of Western Europe and North America now have people from many parts of the world and have adults and children who speak two, three or even more languages.

Is it unusual to be bilingual?

A short answer to this question is: No. In the world generally, it is quite usual for people to use and speak more than one language. In fact, it is more normal than not for people in most parts of the world to speak more than one language. However, in the cities of Western Europe and North America people are having to decide:

how many languages should children learn to use?

should children be encouraged to continue to use the language of the ancestral homelands?

should children be encouraged to learn only the high prestige languages?

should children be raised speaking only one language?

should they concentrate on one language only?

The following pages answer these questions. Feel free to jump from one page to another. Look at the questions that interest you more. There is no harm in reading those parts first.

Should young people be encouraged to use two languages?

There are many arguments for and against that have to be considered before making a decision. The purpose of this book is to bring to you the scientific arguments in straightforward language. So, to find answers to this question, you will have to read other parts of the book.

What does it mean to be bilingual

A bilingual person knows, understands and uses two or more languages. A bilingual person may read and write in the two languages. Does it mean that a person has two separate brains or two separate personalities? Language scientists believe that different languages do not occupy different parts of the brain. The language part of the brain is not made of separate compartments for different languages. Knowledge and experience of language use certain parts of the brain; one whole area is occupied by the experience of languages. So being bilingual means that the brain works in certain ways; there are certain ways the two languages are used, and there are certain ways that the personality develops. These points are discussed in more detail elsewhere in the book.

Home language, mother tongue or first language?

In this book, the language that people use daily in the home is called the *home language*. It can also be called the *mother tongue* but in many families the mother tongue is different from the language that the parents would like their children to learn to read and write. Some educators also talk about *first language* and *second language* in an attempt to explain the difference between the language a child learns to speak first and the language later learnt at school. This is why in English speaking countries many children are said to be learning *English as a Second Language (ESL)* and very often, these children are even called *ESL children*! To be positive and value the two languages that some children have, many teachers prefer to call these children *bilingual,* so acknowledging that they have two languages. Sometimes you will hear about *multilingual schools* or *multicultural schools* because they have pupils who speak different languages and come from different cultures. You might also hear about *multilingual children* who speak more than two languages. Or these children, too, are described as *bilingual.* Sometimes, you will hear the term *Speakers of Languages Other than English.* This is another way of recognising that children who are learning the school language are not without language but have another language or languages they can use. When a child does not speak the school language, some teachers make the mistake of saying that the child has no language! This is why many schools prefer to talk about *Speakers of Languages Other than English (SLOE).*

So in this book, you will read about *home language* to mean the language that is used daily in the home and the language that the parents would like their children to keep using. It also talks about *the language of the school* or the *school language*. In most cases, this would mean English. But the book is also written for families in France, Germany, Holland, and countries where other languages are used to teach school subjects. The book also uses the term: the *language of the larger society*. Also, the phrase *language of the larger society* describes the national languages in France, Germany, Holland and other countries which use their own national language in government, social and political business and in teaching school subjects. This distinguishes the national language from the many other languages spoken by people living in these countries.

Is it normal to be bilingual?

In many parts of the world, children grow up using more than one language. When the language of the streets and the markets is different from the language of the home, children start using these other languages without effort. In many parts of the world, people continue to use these languages in their adult life. Sometimes the language of religion is different from the language used in the home and many children around the world have special lessons to learn the language of their religion. In many countries, the language of the school is different from the language of the home so children have to learn a different language at school. In many parts of the world, more than one language is taught in the school. If we look at the whole world, we see that it is normal for people to use two or more languages.

In most cities today, many different languages are spoken. This is especially true of the cities of Western Europe and North America because people from many parts of the world have come to these cities to make a living. Some children go through life speaking more than one language quite naturally as they grow up. But in some cases, because children are learning a different language at school, they begin to lose the language of their parents as they grow up. The language of the home gets subtracted from a child's ability.

Today it is becoming more and more usual to see families where the mother and father grew up speaking different languages. In some cases, only one parent speaks a language different from the national language and such families generally like their children to grow up speaking the language of the country they are living in and also the parent's language. Some parents are very keen for their children to grow up speaking more than one language so they send them to schools where another language is taught.

Some parents even send their children, at a huge expense, to another country so that their child can learn a second language. In this case, parents are usually interested in their children learning a high prestige language. In situations like this, children usually add a language to the one they speak at home and so grow up speaking two languages.

Ordinary and natural bilingualism

In most parts of the world, people speak more than one language simply because they grow up doing so. Their lives are such that they have to grow up knowing and using more than one language. They may not always be able to read and write all the languages they know. Sometimes, the home language they use does not have a written form but it may have a long history of being used as a spoken language. None the less, people using these languages are bilingual. They may not have studied them at school or college but they are still bilingual. Sadly, this kind of bilingual skill is often thought to be worthless and not even recognised.

With the growing number of people seeking a livelihood in different parts of the world, bilingual people of this kind are growing in number. In all the cities of the world, it is the immigrants and people who have joined the families of these immigrants who grow up naturally speaking more than one language. It is families like these that have to decide if they should help their children grow up with more than one language. To be able to decide, we need to know how children learn languages. It is necessary to know more about the human brain and its connection with language.

THE BRAIN

How many languages can the human brain cope with?

Many people have a strange notion that the human brain has just so much space to store information and no more. Scientists do not know how much a human being can learn or how much information a human mind can store. But it is normal in many parts of the world for people to grow up using two, three or more languages. It seems that people who grow up using only one language are not using all the power of their brain.

The picture on this page illustrates what was once believed about the brain.

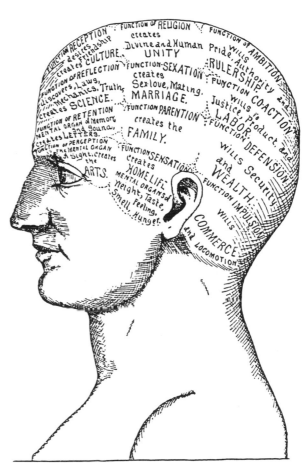

How much information can the brain hold?

How many languages can a child learn?

Scientists and educators do not know exactly how many languages a person can learn. But we do know that in many situations, children pick up languages naturally and without much effort. Many people in the world grow up knowing and using more than one language. There might be the language used in the home, the language used in the school, the language of religion and perhaps the language of the streets and markets. In most parts of the world, different languages are used for these different situations and people grow up using the languages as appropriate.

One thing we can be certain about is that the human brain is not like a jug that can hold so much and no more. It is not as if pouring more information into the brain will make it overflow!

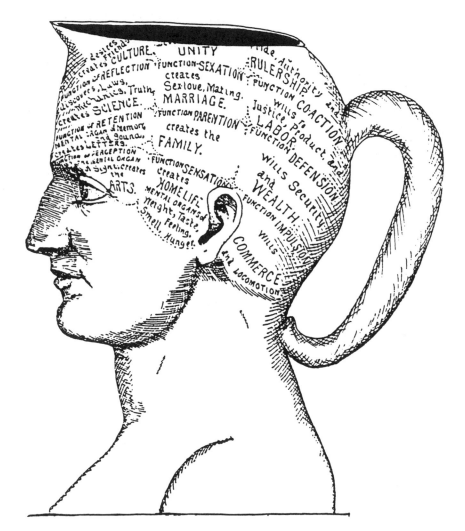

The human brain is not like a jug

Will children get confused if they hear and learn two languages at the same time?

What people might see as confusion is really the way in which children learn to use languages. It also happens when a child is learning one language only. While learning to talk, all children mix up words and sentences. They also invent their own words and sentences. It is over a period of time, after making mistakes and correcting them, that children learn to talk and use language fluently. Of course, when learning to use two languages, a child will mix words and sentences from the two languages. These are not really mistakes but show that a child is learning to use different words and ways of making different sentences. Also, quite quickly, children become aware of the two different languages they use. Very early on, children know the difference between the language that is used with family and friends and the language to be used with teachers and school friends. It is natural for a child to make mistakes when learning to use language — whether one or more. It is the way that they learn.

Children also learn from their mistakes and so do bilingual children. But it is only people who are inexperienced in bilingual language growth who are horrified by these mistakes. The mistakes and mix-ups are a part of growing up and learning to use the languages. But because the child is learning to use two languages, the mistakes and mix-ups are sometimes different from those made by a child learning to use one language. These confusions do not last forever and children who grow up learning two languages soon work out the rules of the two languages. If the two languages are allowed to develop healthily, the child will have the advantage of being strong in not just one but two languages.

Will the two languages interfere with one another in a child's mind?

Teachers and language scientists have talked a good deal about *language interference*. By this they mean that if a child works in two languages, there will be confusion in the child's mind. The two languages will get mixed up. This is not a correct way of looking at language development. Many teachers and language scientists are now paying more attention to *language transference*. This means that what children learn in one language can be useful in learning another. Knowledge that is gained in one language is also useful in learning and developing another language. Knowledge about the grammar and rules of one language is used in developing knowledge of the other.

Naturally, there will be times when words and grammar of the two languages will get confused in a child's mind. But this will pass. Very early on, children understand the difference between the languages they speak, where to speak them, and which language to speak to whom. Children who learn two languages understand better how languages work. They are more able to play with language and find new and interesting ways of using words and language.

Languages in schools around the world

In most countries of the world, it is quite normal for children to learn another language at school from an early age. In schools in France, Germany, Spain, Italy and Denmark, for example, it is quite usual for young children to learn another European language in addition to the national language. It is mainly in the English speaking countries that learning another language is not seen to be of great educational value. However, we must not forget that some rich families encourage their children to learn other languages, send them to schools where languages are taught from an early age, and on expensive holidays to other countries to improve their knowledge of a foreign language. It is children from ordinary families who go to government schools who are usually not given the chance to learn another language. And when they arrive at schools speaking another language, some schools and teachers see it as a problem.

Some schools may teach foreign languages like Russian, Japanese, Mandarin Chinese or even Arabic, because these languages are seen to be economically important. But this happens in only some schools. Not all schools value the teaching of languages to young children. And in many countries, the languages of the people who have come to settle there are valued least of all.

How many alphabets can children cope with?

This is another question parents ask. Can children cope with different writing systems for different languages? Can children learn to use different scripts at the same time? Here again, it should be remembered that in many parts of the world, children grow up using more than one script. Japan is a good example of a country where children grow up learning more than one alphabet.

All school children in Japan grow up learning to read and write Japanese and English. Furthermore, Japanese language itself is made up of three scripts which are quite different from one another. All Japanese children learn KANJI which is related to the Chinese written language. They also learn HIRAGANA which is needed for writing sentences in Japanese and they also learn KATAKANA which is needed to write certain words in the language. So a typical Japanese sentence is made up of three different scripts and children know which script to use for which words.

The three different scripts in a normal Japanese sentence look like this:

Script:	Kanji	Hiragana	Katakana	Hiragana	Kanji	Hiragana
	私	は	ロンドン	に	住	んでいます。
Sound:	*Watakushi*	*wa*	*London*	*ni*	*sun*	*de imasu*
Meaning:	I	(do)	London	in	live	(am)
Translation: I live in London						

All Japanese children, then, grow up learning three quite different scripts and they learn to write the English alphabet too. They also learn Chinese and European numerals. The ideas about confusion in children's minds, and about putting additional burdens on their minds seem to be the worries of teachers and educators who know only one language themselves and are unaware of what is happening in schools around the world. Many readers of this book perhaps grew up learning to read and write two or even more languages.

When schools do not teach or support children's home languages, it may mean that parents will have to teach these languages to their children themselves or send them to language classes run in the communities. It is important that parents do everything possible to make sure that children grow up speaking, reading and writing more than one language. Throughout the book there will be reasons given to support this idea.

Readers of this book who grew up speaking a different language at home and at school will remember that they possibly used two, three or even more languages in their childhood. For example, when I was a child, we used Gujerati at home. My mother and father used Kachchi, a language related to Gujerati, to each other. Sometimes there were visitors in the house, when perhaps Urdu, Hindi or English was spoken. The language of the streets and markets was Swahili. The language of religion was Arabic, and the language of the school was English! At school, I was taught to read and write Gujerati and English and later on, I started learning French at school. Later on in life, I started learning to speak, read and write other languages. This is not unusual — it happens in many parts of the world.

What are the advantages of growing up using more than one language?

A good number of teachers and language scientists believe that keeping and maintaining a child's two languages is a good thing for several reasons. Many also believe that teaching a new language to children who would normally speak only one is good for their mental and educational development. Before discussing the advantages of being bilingual, we need to understand some important points about language and mental development.

Using languages to look at the world

Many teachers and language scientists are of the opinion that children who grow up using two languages are better able to understand how languages work. They can more easily see the difference between how a thing is named and what the thing really is. This is an important skill, needed for logical thinking and for understanding the world. For example, the animal DOG is named differently in different languages but it is still a dog. The name to describe the animal changes but the animal remains the same. People who speak only one language are not always aware that this is so.

Children who grow up using more than one language are also better able to understand that there are different ways of talking about things we experience. There are different ways of talking about time and things that happened in the past. Some languages divide non-living things into male and female. Different languages divide the colours of the rainbow differently. This does not make any one language better or more correct than another. It only shows that there are many sides to reality and that there are different ways of describing things in the world. Take the example of describing family relationships. In English, for example, there are words for aunt, uncle, grandmother or grandfather. These words give information about the relationships but they do not tell us exactly how the people are related. Is the grandmother the mother's mother or the father's mother? Is the aunt the father's sister, the mother's sister or the mother's brother's wife? Many languages have different names for describing maternal and paternal relationships.

In the language I grew up speaking, for example, each of my aunts: my mother's sister, my mother's brother's wife, my father's sister, my father's elder brother's wife and my father's younger brother's wife have different titles! So in my home language, Gujerati, I have five different words for aunts who are related to me in five different ways. Also, there are different words to describe uncles, nieces and nephews related in a particular way. I do not remember ever being confused about these different relationships and the titles for them. Many languages have additional ways of describing and speaking to relations who are older or younger. A child who knows all the different words for these relationships is not confused. That child, in fact, has more words to describe and understand these relationships.

PEANUTS

The wealth of languages

The advantages of speaking two languages can only be gained if a child's bilingual development has been positive and healthy. Many children grow up feeling ashamed of their home language. They feel that the schools and the outside world do not recognise their home language and they may even grow up thinking that their language is inferior or useless. Children who have been made to feel this way might lose their mother tongue. Although they first use the language of the home, the language of the school develops more and more as they go through school, and their home language develops less and less. The home language can disappear after a few years at school. Language scientists call this *Subtractive Bilingualism*. But when children grow up learning the language of the school and society and at the same time develop their home language, language scientists call this *Additive Bilingualism*. These children add a language to the one they already know. They don't lose anything.

Helping children keep their languages will help them become richer in languages, culture and certain things that a speaker of only one language cannot easily appreciate. By helping children to speak, read and write other languages, parents will be helping them to use more of their brain power and making it easier for them to learn and understand other languages. What is more, they will be able to speak to their elders and understand more of their philosophies, music, arts and other areas of knowledge that depend on language. They will be able to visit their ancestral homelands without feeling and behaving like foreigners. They may have even greater opportunities in business and intellectual life because they are able to speak the language of their original homeland and culture. In the long run, it will also enable children to feel good about themselves and be proud of who they are.

To appreciate the other advantages of using two languages we also need to understand what is meant by being *good at languages*.

Being good at languages — What does it mean?

Certain people have very strange ideas about what being good at languages or being bilingual means. These ideas come from monolingual people.

What language do you dream in?

One such idea is that we do not really speak a language well unless we think in it or we start dreaming in it. This idea does not fit with what we know about using language for thinking. Scientists today believe that the language we use for speaking and the language we use for thinking are quite different. There are many bilingual people who think in one language, the other or both. It depends on what they are thinking about. As for dreaming, scientists believe that dreaming takes place not through languages but through ideas. This is why in dreams, a whole story or an event is sometimes seen in a flash. Languages only come into dreams when the dream is about languages or when an actual conversation takes place in the dream. Even then, the language part of the dream can pass in a flash and is not always played out like a tape recorder!

Which language do you think in?

Imagine that you are going to enter a room full of people. The moment you come through the door, you have a pretty good idea about many of the people you recognise, people you like, people you dislike or positively hate! You have also decided which part of the room you are going to and where you would like to sit. If you were doing all this thinking in your ordinary language, you would be frozen at the doorway looking quite stupid! Most of us do all this thinking almost in a flash. All this thinking seems to be done in a quick form of language. This is the language of thought and it works faster than spoken language. But there are also times when people use ordinary language to go through certain steps in their thinking — for example, when they are thinking aloud. But this way of thinking is different and takes longer. It is more like talking to oneself. Many bilingual people will do different kinds of thinking in one language or the other. For example, some people count in their home language or in the language they first learnt at school. Some may count the smaller numbers in the language they learnt first and do the counting of the higher numbers in the language they used in school.

Many bilingual people use both their languages to do their thinking. Which they use depends on what they are thinking about. They may think about their emotions or loved ones in the language of their childhood. They may think about their studies or work in their other language. Children who grow up in homes where their father and mother each speak different languages, may use the two languages to think about different things. In short, there is no one simple rule about which language a bilingual person uses in doing their thinking. The use of their two languages depends on when they started learning each of the languages. Did their mother and father come from different language backgrounds? Was one language used by the parents and the older members of the family but another used with the children? Was the other language learnt at school or was it learnt naturally by hearing and using it with the people around? It also depends on what is being thought about and if the thinking is about people. It is not easy to say which language is used in thinking. There are different possibilities for different people.

Bilingual people use their languages to do different kinds of thinking. Just think about the language you use for talking to your mother or father, the language you use with your friends and the language you will use for talking to your teacher. Those people who grew up using two languages will perhaps agree that they will use their two different languages in different situations. But even people who grew up using one language will perhaps agree that the kind of language they would use in talking to their family or close friends will be different from the kind of language they would use with their teacher or employer or with people who are more distant.

Speaking like a native — what does that mean?

There are certain monolinguals who believe that bilingual people cannot speak either of their two languages as well as those who speak only one. Some language scientists talk about '*speaking like a native*'. They believe that bilingual speakers will never speak like a native in either of the two languages. This idea does not hold up. First of all, speaking a language has many parts. There are the sounds, the words, the grammar, the rhythm and the music of the language. Then there are different functions: friendly talk, serious talk, telling stories, telling jokes, playing with words. Different people are good at doing different things. They cannot all do all the things equally well. So it is difficult to say what speaking like a native really means. Some people are good at some things and not others. Bilingual people may be good at some things in one of their languages and not the other.

Does speaking like a native mean making no mistakes?

All people make mistakes when they speak. If we listen to a tape recording of some natural speech, made even by an educated speaker, it is surprising to hear how many grammatical mistakes there are! Sentences are left unfinished, the beginning of a sentence does not match the ending, some sentences start in one period of time and finish in another. This is quite usual in free, natural speech. A bilingual speaker also makes these mistakes. But because a bilingual person may also mix sounds and words of the other language, this is noticed immediately by monolingual people. The mistakes that monolingual people make while speaking are noticed less or not at all.

Some bilingual people can speak, read, write and think equally well in both their languages. Language scientists call these people *balanced bilinguals*.

Mixing languages — does it mean you are not good at a language?

It is known that bilingual people mix words from their two languages when they are speaking to other bilinguals like themselves. These are not mistakes. Language scientists call this *code mixing*. Sometimes, people who speak two languages mix sentences or start a sentence in one language and finish it in another. This is called *code switching*. It does not mean that bilingual people do not know their two languages. They only speak like this to other bilingual speakers like themselves. Sometimes, young children may mix or switch codes with speakers of one language, like their teachers or friends at school, but they quickly learn when to stop doing so. Sometimes bilingual people may slip into the other language, but usually they do so with people who speak the same two languages. Generally, bilingual people know very well which language to use and when — they are very good at getting this right.

Listen to a bilingual person speaking on the telephone. When the phone call is about work or with a monolingual person, it is all in one language. If the call is to a close friend or family member who is also bilingual, the person will probably switch from one language to another. In fact, language scientists believe that the two languages of a bilingual person are not separate but make one continuous whole. A bilingual person uses one, the other or a mixture of both, depending on the subject matter and with whom the language is being used. A bilingual person is able to move easily from one language to another.

So when a bilingual person mixes the two languages and switches from one language to another, we are wrong to think that the person is making mistakes. These are the ways that bilingual people use their two languages.

Is it wrong to use your home language in public?

Bilingual people have a choice of which language to use with other bilingual people. Quite often, they do so without thinking. For example, with close friends and family members, it is quite natural to use the home language. Sometimes, when bilingual people want to indicate that they do not wish to become close to a person, they might speak in the language of the school or the language of the larger society. This could happen in a shop when, although the shopper and the shopkeeper know that they both speak the same languages, they choose to speak in the language of the larger society. On the other hand, there may be times when a bilingual speaker chooses to use the home language of the shopkeeper to get friendlier service! Which of the two languages a bilingual speaker uses depends on different situations.

Sometimes in public, bilingual people are reluctant to use their home language when there are members of the larger society around. The larger society has made bilingual speakers feel guilty, ashamed or diffident about using their language in public. Why should this be so? People will always have private and personal things to talk about in public. They may whisper, use their eyes, hands and facial expressions to talk about private and personal things. It is no business of anybody who might happen to be nearby. When the conversation has nothing to do with the people around, it should not matter what language the speakers use. However, this sometimes becomes a problem at work. Most people in modern cities are aware that people use different languages and most leave them alone. Some people even find the many languages of the modern city exciting and interesting. Unfortunately, there are some people who think that when someone uses another language in their presence, this is being rude. Certain people are hostile to other languages, feeling that:

This is my country. We speak English (or French, or German) here. You are a newcomer here. How dare you use your language in my presence!

When I am told: 'It is rude to speak in your language', my answer is: 'It is rude to listen to other people's conversation!' The situation is not an easy one. Most people do not want to be awkward or different. They just stop using their language in public. The problem is often with speakers of the language of the larger society who feel that bilingual people have no right to use their other language in public. These monolinguals feel unnecessarily powerless when they cannot understand the other language. This can be true of teachers who hear children in the classroom speaking in another language and feel uncomfortable because they feel that they should be in control of what language people around them should use!

With these kind of attitudes from monolingual people, it is not surprising to hear that some studies of bilingual people have even claimed that bilingual people are dishonest, cunning, unreliable or of lower intelligence!

Is there any proof that bilingualism is an advantage?

Many studies have followed the progress of a large number of bilingual children over a period of years. A good number of these studies show that children who experience positive bilingual learning do better at school. Look at the summaries of some of these important research studies given on pages 43 to 47. Many teachers and language scientists think that those who speak two languages find it easier to learn even more languages. It is no accident that many bilingual speakers around the world also know other languages.

Many bilingual people do not even think about this ability they have. A large number of children in many countries of Asia, Africa and Latin America and in parts of Europe and the United States of America grow up using more than two languages.

Can it be said that mathematics is another language? It would be interesting to see if people who speak more than one language are also better at maths. Certainly, some researchers have shown that bilingual children are better able to think in totally new directions. Educationists call this kind of thinking *divergent thinking*.

But apart from school subjects, there are other issues that are important for the well-being of bilingual children. These are to do with the *self-esteem* and confidence that bilingual children have in themselves. Self-esteem and pride also effect how much they succeed at school and in their studies. A child who is happy with himself or herself is also likely to be happy with school and studying.

What do bilingual children think of themselves?

A language that a child has grown up with is important for the child's personality. The affection and care that the child gets from parents and family, but mostly from the mother, is expressed in the home language. Early experiences of love, pleasure, joy and the things that are important to the child happen in the home language. Later on, giving names to foods, relatives and other things around the child is also in the home language.

But when the school and the outside world tells children, in many ways, that the language that they are most intimate and familiar with is worthless, they have to make difficult adjustments. When children are made to feel that their language, their food, their way of living, even their names are not quite normal, is it not a miracle that many go through school and society keeping their self-confidence and dignity? They might be teased, bullied and even beaten for being who they are and this may explain why some might want to change their names, or refuse to talk in the home language, or even refuse to eat the customary food of the household.

So what can parents do? Some parents understandably come to think that it is best to encourage their children to speak, live and behave like members of the larger society. These parents unthinkingly tell children the same negative things about their own language and culture that the schools, teachers and the larger society tell them: the culture and the language of the larger society are more valuable than the culture and language of their home.

Taking pride in your language

All parents would like their children to succeed at school and be good at the language of the school. But abandoning all the things that makes an individual is no solution. People can take on the food, language, clothes, mannerisms and even a name from the majority society but if they look different, that society will still regard them as 'different'. What a pity if after all, people lose their identity and are still considered not equal! Does it not make better sense for them to be as good as anybody else in the language of the majority society, accept their food, clothes and habits but continue to be who they are, too, and make sure that their rights are respected and that they are treated as equals? It is enriching to keep things from one's own culture and add positive things from others'. By doing this, people can keep their self-respect and dignity. They also become richer in languages, experience, skills and culture.

The culture of any nation or society is made up of the cultures of all the people who are part of it. Each person should feel confident that their own culture is a part of the national culture and children should be encouraged to be richer in cultures, and not poorer by adopting only some parts of the culture of a society. Similarly, by continuing to use and develop their home language, people can take pride in their language and so take pride in themselves. Doing so gives children the chance to take pride in themselves and become richer in culture and languages.

Language and ancestral roots

Those of us who are raising young children are doing so at an important stage in history. Studies of the histories of groups of people who left their homelands to settle elsewhere have shown that the first generation settlers continue to use their home language. It is the second generation that tends to use the home language less and less with their children. Knowingly or unknowingly, the larger society makes it very difficult for the new settlers to continue to use it. But it is usually the children of the third and fourth generations who begin to ask questions about their identity. Sometimes, within the same generation, when they have already lost their language and home culture, some young people begin to ask questions about their own identity, culture and languages when they grow up.

This happened in USA. For example, people of Jewish, Polish, Greek or Italian origin changed their names, language and food habits to become part of American society. Nearly a hundred years later, people realised the disadvantages of losing or hiding their background, as they had done because the larger society had put pressure on them to stop being different. Today, many are going back to using their original names and teaching their children their original language and cultures, after denying or hiding them for years. Naturally, it is not easy to go back to the language and culture given up generations ago. Even so, many people in United States are making efforts to get back what they have lost. Should we not learn from the mistakes of others instead of repeating them?

3

HOME AND SCHOOL

In many homes today, parents use one language between themselves but speak the language of the school with their children. Or parents may speak to their children in their home language and the children reply in the language of the school. The children may have spoken the home language when they were very young but when they start going to school, they use their home language less and less. There are many reasons why this happens.

How many languages should a child learn to become successful?

All parents are concerned about their children's progress in school. Many parents would like their children to continue to use and learn the home language but want to make sure that their children succeed in school. We all know that to succeed in school, children should be able to speak, read and write the language of the school as well as the other children do. The language of the school is also the one that matters in society and the larger world. Some parents are afraid that the home language is of little value. Some believe that the home language is only useful in keeping in touch with the home culture. Some think that they will first encourage their children to be good at the language of the school and start teaching the home language later on. They believe that their child will become confused by learning two languages. They may also think that learning two or more languages is a burden on the child and that the brain cannot cope with more than one. This book has shown that this is not true.

It does not help that certain teachers and schools advise parents to speak the language of the school at home. This is certainly not good advice for parents who are not fluent in the language of the school. Research by language scientists and educators shows that it is not *which language* but *what kind of things and the way* in which parents speak to their children that is important for their educational progress.

Research also shows that children who have a strong foundation in their home language are better able to learn reading and writing in the language of the school. Teachers have noticed that it is easier for children to learn reading and writing if they already know about reading and writing in their home language.

For children to be successful at school and in life, they certainly need to be good at the language of the school and the larger society but this does not mean that they have to stop using and developing the language of the home. Quite the opposite.

Which language should be used in the home?

It is very important to talk to children about all the different things around them and about their lives. The things they see, the questions they ask, the printed things they read. In short, all the experiences of a child could become the topic for interesting discussions. This is known to be good for the mental and educational development of children. Reading to your child is also important. When parents read to their children regularly, their children grow to enjoy books and enjoy reading and become better readers. Similarly, songs and stories are important for a child's mental and educational development. All these activities could be done in the languages that the parents speak daily in the home. There is no rule that says that it should be only in the language of the school.

What if schools do not value the language of the home?

Many teachers and schools do regard your and your child's languages positively. They know that the languages and experience that your child brings to school are worthwhile. They are delighted when they see that a child can use two or more languages and they may well allow them to be used in the classroom. In such an environment, children will feel secure and happy to hear their home languages in the classroom, not feel ashamed or different. All this is good for their self-confidence. Some schools even encourage children to develop their home languages. Parents who are lucky enough to find schools like these should help the schools to keep it up. But not all schools can help children to read, write and develop their home languages so it might have to be done at home by parents. Parents who do not feel confident in the school language would do well to learn it from their children while they teach them the home language. This way, there will be positive learning experiences for everyone in the home.

Unfortunately, some schools are not happy about children speaking mainly their home language and not the language of the school. There are schools and teachers who think that this means more work for them. Although they do not actually say it, they make the parents accept that their children will only benefit from the school system if they arrive speaking the language of the school. And because parents want the best for their children, they do not question this. Also, they worry about what might happen if their children are not feeling well? What if they want to go to the toilet? What if they have a problem of some kind? Will the children be able to explain? Will the teacher understand? These are real worries but the answer does not lie in taking a language away from your child. The answer lies in bringing about changes in the value given to languages in the home and at school.

A child's world

For many years, schools and teachers have worked in a *child-centred* way. This means that learning and teaching is based on the child's world of experience. This is a good way of teaching because people can only increase their knowledge by building upon what they already know — and that is true of all learning at whatever age. We saw that knowledge is not something that you pour into a child's mind. Knowledge and learning are developed from experience and the ability to use each experience to make sense of new ones.

As parents, we should be confident that what our children have learnt before going to school is valuable and useful, and this includes the experience of their home language and culture. Parents should make a point of going into schools and taking part in what is going on in the classroom and should offer to help with the children in the class who speak other languages. Most schools would welcome you and most teachers would support you and work with you for your child's progress. Some schools have teachers and helpers who speak the language of the children. If not, it should be suggested to the school that teachers and helpers who know about the language and the culture of the children should be employed.

The language of the school in the home

In some families, children speak to their mothers and grandparents in the home language but use the school language with their fathers. The daily home activities: I am hungry, I am tired, pass me the salt, and so on, are usually said to mother or the grandparent, in the home language. But when talking about television programmes, video games, homework, cars and so on, it is usually with the father — and not discussed in the home language. Without ever having talked about it, the child very quickly learns that the ordinary things in life can be discussed in the home language but that the important and scientific things are discussed in the school language and very often with the men in the house! Important and interesting television programmes, bright books and magazines are all in the language of the school. The teachers use the language of the school. In fact, most things that matter in the growing child's world happen in the language of the school.

Parents who are trying to help their children to grow up using two languages are faced with huge competition and will have to do a lot of thinking and planning to help their children become bilingual. It is not enough just telling your child to speak in the home language. That is not going to work. Some of the things that parents can do in the home to encourage the use of two languages are discussed on pages 40 to 42 and in other parts of this book.

When one language takes over

In some homes, children use both the home language and the language of the school. However, very soon, the child's development in the language of the school begins to get well ahead of the home language, because, after the child enters school, almost all of the building of knowledge takes place in the school language. Most schools ignore the home language completely. In some schools, the home language is used a little — but only to help children to learn the language of the school. So as soon as they start using the school language, they are discouraged from using their home language at school. When children start going to school, they spend more of their active hours with teachers and children who speak the language of the school than they spend hearing and using their home language. So it is easy to understand why the school language is likely to develop more than the home language.

This book is not suggesting that parents should *not* encourage children to be good at the school language. Of course, everyone has to be good at the language of the larger society if they want to succeed. But the question is this:

Can children's home language be maintained and developed without harming their progress in the school language?

A short answer is this:

There is proof that a child using more than one language has advantages in thinking and studying. But there is no proof that keeping and developing the home language harms a child's progress in the school.

Parents should have confidence that it is possible for children to grow up being good at the language of the school and also at the language of the home. It is interesting to see that some of the world's best recognised writers of recent years are themselves bilingual.

4

SOCIETY

How can society make you lose your language?

No child wants to be different from other children. They want to speak the language spoken by the other children in the school. They want to eat the food other children eat. They want to wear the same clothes, listen to the same music and do the things that young people like them do. They want to belong and be the same. If they are different, life can be very difficult. They will not be able to make friends, others will laugh at them or bully them or pick fights with them. This *peer group pressure* happens in any school. It is a fact of life for young people. They would rather die than wear shoes that are not just the right fashion! They would rather die than eat food that is different!

Television, newspapers and magazines make full use of this peer pressure to make children want to buy only certain kinds of things and insist on particular brand names on clothes, shoes, toys, games and food. Matters are made more difficult for children who look different, speak a different language at home, eat food that is different and whose parents may wear clothes that come from a different part of the world.

These children have to cope with something much more complicated than mere peer group pressure and advertisements. We hear stories about how children would throw away the food their mothers had packed for them rather than eat it at school. They would starve and not tell anyone. There are stories of how even at home, children will not eat the food that the family eats. And of course, they will not speak the language of the home and, if they do know it, they will be embarrassed to use it outside the home. Children will tell their teachers that they do not speak their home language. It is only when schools and society start valuing other languages that children will be proud to be heard speaking them. Educators now know that children as young as three years old are aware of racial differences. Even at that age, children know that society values certain people and cultures more than others. Although there is far less peer group pressure at this young age, some children will not speak with their parents in their home language outside the home.

To add to the problem, many parents have made this a part of their own thinking. They are reluctant or embarrassed to speak their own language in public. In shops and restaurants, some parents will not speak to their children in their home language. Some even feel proud when their children cannot speak the home language. Perhaps they feel that by forgetting the home language, their child has really become part of the larger society. This is understandable, because for generations, many parents have believed that speaking English, German or French is a sign of being well-educated. But look how strange the situation can be. Canada is officially a bilingual country. Politicians and people who work for the government are required to speak, read and write both English and French. In certain jobs, people who speak English and French are given a 'bilingual bonus' — extra money in their pay. So French has economic value. Yet in certain parts of Canada, people do not consider French to be a high status language. Speaking in French is not seen by everyone as sign of being well-educated. Some people in Canada consider French to be of lower value and some children in Canada are ashamed to be heard speaking in French! So it is actually society that makes certain languages of less value, even when these languages have respect and value elsewhere in the world.

How can you tell when children are ashamed of their home culture?

At restaurants with their parents, some children will not eat the food their parents eat, saying that the food is too hot and spicy or that they do not like it. Of course, we all know how children will dislike certain foods and refuse to eat them! We all know children who prefer certain fast foods — hamburgers and pizzas — and from certain shops only! But the problem is not simply a matter of children's likes and dislikes. In many cases it is because children are ashamed of their culture and food habits. For example, in the USA and Canada today, Mexican food is very fashionable and is available in many food stalls and fast food restaurants. Although it can be quite hot and spicy, children will eat it because it is fashionable. It is funny to see children from India and Pakistan who will not eat their home cooking, happily eating spicy Mexican food! But society sends mixed messages to children. It may be fashionable for grownups to eat Chinese or Indian food, for example, but some people make unpleasant jokes about these foods. Jokes of this kind are repeated at school and children from these or other home cultures are made to feel inferior and ashamed of themselves. Here then, are young children who are pushed by pressure to be the same as other children, and made to feel ashamed of who they are. Their parents will need to think hard and plan what to do if they want their children to feel good about themselves and succeed in life.

How parents can give negative messages about their home language

Hidden messages

Children learn many things by seeing how adults behave. Many speakers of other languages do not value their own language themselves. Children know from the actions and behaviour of adults that the language of the home is valued less than the language of the larger society. Moreover, children can see that the important things in life are done in the language of the larger society. They learn this very early in their lives and make it a part of their thinking. Parents may have to change their own behaviour and ideas if they want their children to value their home language. It is not enough just telling children this or lecturing to them about how valuable the home language is and that it should not be forgotten. Simply talking about it is not going to work. Parents and other adults will have to do certain things to make children proud and comfortable about their language and culture. Look at pages 40 to 42 for ideas for positive things to do to give value to home language and encourage its use in the home.

Happy families

Of course, there are also the children who go to restaurants with their parents and do enjoy the food that belongs to their home culture. Some children are quite happy to talk with their parents in their home language in public and the parents are equally comfortable talking to their children in their home language in the outside world. In some families, children see that their parents and elders genuinely value their home language and culture. It would be interesting to see what parents and young people do in these families to support a healthy development of home languages.

Mothering children

It is now thought that children start listening to the sounds of a language even before they are born. Certainly, the sounds that babies hear in the months after they are born are important for their mental and language development. Yet many times, mothers feel that they cannot talk and play in their home language with their new baby while they are in the hospital. They may try to talk to their baby in the language of the larger society but might not know how to, because their own mothers had only spoken to them in their home language. What about the songs we sing to babies? Some mothers are too ashamed of their language and culture to want to sing them in the hospital. Many mothers just keep quiet until they get home.

Monolingual pressure

We can see how English-speaking countries regard other languages by seeing what they think about teaching other languages to children. Teaching other languages to young children is generally not thought to be important. If another language is taught, it is usually a European language like French or Spanish. But other European countries value teaching languages to young children, although usually the other important languages of Europe. So, for example, schoolchildren in Spain may learn English and French and schoolchildren in France may learn English.

Parents should support schools that teach languages to children. But not many schools will be prepared to teach children's home languages in school. One way of encouraging schools to recognise and value home languages is for parents to continue using them with children. If parents are positive about their home languages, the schools will be more likely to recognise and value them. Parents should be confident about keeping up their home languages and not pressured into giving them up. When the larger society tells parents to use one language only and forget their home language, it is like the story of the fox that had lost its tail.

One day, wandering in the forest, a fox accidentally got its tail cut off.

It looked rather funny and was very embarrassed. Then it had an idea. It called a conference of all the animals. When it had gathered all the animals together, it told them how wonderful and clever it was for all of us to cut off our tails.

The animals thought that what the fox was telling them was very strange. They liked their tails. They found their tails very useful for doing all kinds of things.

Thinking a little more about it, they decided to not listen to the fox and to keep their tails. So in the end, the fox was the only animal that didn't have a tail!

What can be done if schools do not value home languages?

Parents have to continue to impress upon the school authorities that they value their home language and would like their children to continue to use it. If parents show confidence and pride in their own languages, the school may start to respect their languages. One important way of doing this is to teach the languages at home or support language classes in the community. This will also show the children that parents consider it important to continue to learn and use home languages.

Until the schools and teachers do take home languages seriously, parents have to continue to find ways of encouraging the use of their language in the home, and ways of developing speaking, reading and writing it with their children. This may mean setting up language teaching classes in the neighbourhood or community. In some communities, language classes have existed for a long time and they should be valued and supported. These classes show schools that parents and communities consider their home languages valuable and worth maintaining. Look at pages 40 to 42 for the kind of activities that parents can do in the home to support and value home languages.

All schools believe that it is important for parents to be more involved with their children's schools and education. Parents should use this opportunity and go into schools to impress upon teachers that they consider their home languages to be important, useful and valuable for their children and that *more* languages should be taught to *all* children.

Should parents send children to language classes in the community?

As long as schools do not teach home languages, parents have little choice. If they would like their children to learn the home language, they should either teach it to them at home themselves or send them to language classes. Children might well resent having to go to language classes on Saturdays or Sundays or in the evenings, when they could be doing other things. Also, there is often a big difference between what children experience in the school classroom and in the language and culture classes run by the communities. The schools and halls where these classes are held become cold and unfriendly out of school hours. The materials and books that are used are not always attractive. Children also realise that they are having to come to these classes because their school does not value their language enough to teach it during school time. The teachers are different and often have a formal and old-fashioned teaching style. This can mean that parents face strong competition and have to ask their children to do something they do not always enjoy. So although it is a good idea to send children to language classes in the community, ways have to be found to make these classes modern and enjoyable for the children.

How can language classes be made more enjoyable?

First of all, it has to be remembered that almost all teachers in community language classes work for little or no payment. They do it out of love and concern for their language. These teachers also need to be acknowledged and supported. The work that they have been doing in the communities, often for many years, is very valuable. Ways should be found for the education authorities to make these language classes friendly and modern and teachers should be given training and rewarded for their voluntary work. These teachers need to be helped to develop teaching materials that are as good as those used in the schools for other subjects and to be guided about new ways of teaching. Fortunately, teachers are now coming out of colleges who also teach in the language classes and they are aware of new developments in language teaching. When teaching materials like videos, films, computer programmes, well-produced textbooks and interesting stories and reading material are used in the classes, children will find them far more interesting, enjoyable and worthwhile.

Language and religion

Many parents would like their children to continue with their home language because they see that its use is connected with their religion. They would like their children to keep in touch with both. Once again, parents are faced with competition from other activities like sports, hobbies and computers. If children are pulled away from such activities they can start disliking their language and religion classes. If the choice is between lessons in language or in religion then, in my opinion, parents should concentrate on teaching language first.

Religion can be taught privately at home by parents. If children are in touch with their home language, they will be helped to understand their home culture and religion. This way, they will have time to take part in sports and hobbies too, which are also important for the child's mental and physical development.

Language works!

While parents are waiting for the schools to start teaching home languages, the only way to make sure that their children are not deprived of this valuable heritage is to continue to teach and support these languages in the homes and community. The fact that there is a long and healthy history of language classes run by the communities shows that there are many families that value their languages. They are teaching their home language to their children in the face of all the difficulties and challenges. There are many children in Europe and North America who do grow up using their home languages. But a lot depends on you — as parents, care givers, elders and young people in the community.

5

THE FUTURE

In the modern world, many people find themselves making a living far from the country where they were born. Many families who use one language at home have learnt to use the language of the country they are living in. In some countries, the language of the home is valued and taught in schools. In others, the language of the home is ignored by the schools. Some parents find themselves in communities where it is possible to continue to use and teach the home language to children. But some parents and families might be isolated, so either continue to use and teach the home language privately or start losing it. In some countries, the government and schools are very supportive and provide help and money to teach home languages — sometimes in schools during school time, and sometimes outside school hours. In some countries, less and less money is spent on education and as the home languages are seen to be of little or no value, they have no support from schools or government. In some countries, the other languages are hated and parents and children are forced to stop using them! So parents and children in different countries find themselves in different situations. But the question they have to ask is still the same:

Should the home language be taught to children?

I hope that you have read enough of the book to decide that it is a good idea for children to speak several languages. In most European countries and North America, English, French, German, Spanish are taught in schools. Some schools even teach Russian, Chinese, Arabic or Japanese, because these languages are seen to be of economic value. If children are lucky enough to be in schools like these, parents should certainly encourage their children to learn one or more of these languages. But when families already have another language that they use at home, does it not make sense to enable children to speak it, too, and become better at it? This is true for languages which are written and languages that are only spoken. It is also true of families where the mother and father have different home languages. It is true of families that have lost the language of their ancestors but would like to start learning it again. A question that parents often ask is:

What economic value does my language have?

In 1985, the Department of Education of the USA published a list of 169 languages which the government considered critical. This meant that knowledge of these 169 languages would enable the United States to carry out important scientific research and compete internationally in trade and business. These languages would also help the military power of the United States. A special fund was set up to encourage young people to learn these languages at colleges and universities.

Look at the list of languages. See if your home language is on the list. Ask the children and young people in the home to join you in finding their home language on the list. You might be pleased and surprised to see that the language you speak daily in your home is considered to be of great scientific, military and economic importance by a powerful nation.

Yet some parents consider their own home language worthless and a waste of time to learn. Is it not strange that parents and families do not consider it worth passing on this valuable skill to their children? Is it not strange that many schools do not value the knowledge and skill that parents and children bring to school?

Languages considered to be of economic value by the government of USA

From: The Cambridge Encyclopaedia of Language, David Crystal, Cambridge University Press, 1989

Achinese	Buryat	Gurani	Kpelle	Mundari-Ho	Santali	Songa
Acholi	Cambodian	Gujerati	Krio	Nahuatl	Serbo-Croatian	Tungus
Afrikaans	Catalan	Haitian Creole	Kumauni	Neo-Melanesian	Shona	Turkish
Akan	Chinese	Hausa	Kurdish	Nepali	Sindhi	Turkmen
Albanian	Chuvash	Hebrew	Lahnda	Newari	Sinhalese	Tuvinian
Amharic	Ciokwe	Hindi	Lamani	Ngala	Slovak	Uighur
Arabic	Czech	Hmong	Latvian	Norwegian	Slovene	Ukrainian
Armenian	Danish	Hungarian	Lithuanian	Nyanja	Somali	Urdu
Assamese	Dari	Iban	Luba	Oriya	Songhai	Uzbek
Aymara	Dinka	Icelandic	Macedonian	Oromo	Sotho	Vietnamese
Azerbaijani	Dutch	Igbo	Madurese	Panjabi	Spanish	Visayan
Bahasa Indonesia	Efik	Ilocano	Maithili	Papiamento	Sudanese	Wolof
Balinese	Eskimo	Irish	Malagasy	Pashto	Swahili	Yakut
Baluchi	Estonian	Italian	Malayalam	Persian	Swedish	Yao
Bamileke	Ewe-Fon	Japanese	Manchu	Polish	Tagalog	Yiddish
Bashkir	Fijian	Javanese	Mandekan	Polynesian	Tajik	Yoruba
Basa (Kru)	Finnish	Kamba	Manipuri	Portuguese	Tamil	Yucatec
Belorussian	French	Kannada	Marathi	Quechua	Tatar	Zapotec
Bemba	Fulani	Kanuri	Maya	Rappang	Telegu	Zulu-Xhosa
Bengali	Ga	Kashmiri	Mende	Romanian	Temen	
Berber	Ganda	Kazakh	Minangkabau	Romany	Thai-Lao	
Bhojpuri	Gbaya	Kikuyu	Mixtec	Rundi	Tibetan	
Bikol	Georgian	Kirghiz	Mongolian	Russian	Tigrinya	
Bulgarian	German	Kongo	Mordvin	Rwanda	Tiv	
Burmese	Greek	Korean	More	Sango	Toba Batak	

What kind of things can parents do in the home to support home languages?

Parents can do much to give value to their home language. The following pages give some ideas for parents to try out in the home. Parents should also talk to other families to see what they do at home to support home language.

Talking

Talking to children about things that are interesting and important is an essential part of learning to use a language. Parents should make a habit of talking to their children about everything that happens in their lives: what they see, hear, smell and taste, what they like doing, reading, writing, singing, playing, eating, talking about and so on — the list can be endless. Many parents already do this and they know how good they and their child can become at making conversation. If parents continue with the habit of talking in the home language, a child will grow up knowing that the home language has a use and value and is an important part of their relationship at home.

Reading and writing

All schools and teachers will support you if you read regularly to your child. It is known that children become readers much sooner if their parents read regularly to them. They also grow up enjoying reading and liking books. Reading to children should be a regular and a normal part of the life of a child at home, whatever the age of the child. The joys of reading can be taught to children from a very early age. Parents could start reading in the home language. It is becoming easier to find good and attractive books in a good many languages. There are bookshops that specialise in selling books in many languages. There are also books that have only pictures and no written words, and are meant for making up stories with children. The stories can be told in any language parents want to use. Parents can even write their own stories in these books. There are also books that have the same story written in two languages — bilingual texts — with lively pictures.

Children also love to make stories and story books themselves. Making and writing story books in the home will help children to read, write and develop their languages. They could make their storybooks in their home language.

Stories and songs

Telling stories and singing songs are other activities that help children to develop languages. These days, it is becoming easier to find records and tapes of songs and stories in many languages and parents can make their own tapes of songs and stories. Elders in the family can be asked to make tapes of songs and stories, which will help to develop a special relationship between children and elders in the family.

Elders in the family

In some families children have lost their home language so they cannot talk with their grandparents and older relatives. It is sad to see children losing not only their language but also their contact with their elders. Involving elders in teaching their home language to children will help to strengthen relationships. Children can be encouraged and helped to write letters to elders in the family. Birthdays, festivals and other family news would be good subjects to write about. Children who cannot write in their home language could exchange recorded tapes with family and friends. Visits to the home country also help children to understand the culture and language of the home better.

Books, films and videos

It is becoming easier to find good videos, films and picture books in the different languages. Until recently, many books and pictures from the home countries were poorly produced and not attractive to children. But today there is a range of good books and videos to choose from. Some come from the countries where these languages are widely spoken. But parents will have to be careful that these videos and books fit with what children are being taught at school. For example, schools prefer books and pictures in which boys and girls, men and women, are shown doing similar things. Girls can be doctors, they can repair cars, they can fly aeroplanes, be fire-fighters and so on. It is not only boys who can do these things. If the videos and picture books in the home languages say something different, then children may doubt their value of the home language and culture. If children are to grow up with a healthy outlook on their home culture and home languages, the books and videos in home languages must also have a healthy outlook. Books and videos that show women or other groups of people or other cultures and customs as inferior, go against the teaching for equality and respect for cultures that children should be developing in their education.

Computers

It is becoming easier these days to find computer programmes in different languages and programmes that can write the letters of different languages. If children see that their home language can be produced on the computer, it helps them to realise that their language is modern and as good as the other highly valued languages. Using computers at home can also help children to be good at school work.

Art, music and dance

Encouraging children to develop an interest in artistic activities of the home culture, like learning to sing, dance or play a special musical instrument, will also help them to be positive about themselves and take interest in their home language. They will also meet other young people who like similar things and speak the same languages. The same could be said for other cultural activities like martial arts, sports and calligraphy.

Children as teachers

Parents who are not fluent in the language of the school or the larger society could learn from their children while they are teaching them the home language. This relationship of learning and teaching is a healthy one and will make children feel good about themselves. Children can also be found pen-pals in the country where the home language is spoken so that they can write to each other in their two languages.

6

INTERNATIONAL STUDIES ON BILINGUALISM

In the last twenty years, there have been a good many studies and reports about the advantages of bilingual education. A summary of some of the major studies is given below. Most of them ran over at least five years. The shorter studies also show the advantages of bilingual education but including all the short studies would make the list very long indeed.

The summaries of the various studies are based on work by Jim Cummins, who works mainly in Canada but is known around the world for his studies on bilingualism and language teaching. A summary of his book, *Bilingualism and Special Education*, will be found on page 55.

While reading about these studies, just imagine what would happen if similar studies had been carried out in the country where you are living and the two languages were the language of the larger society and your home language. What would happen to your child's development in the home language and the school language if this kind of education was available to your child?

The **Manitoba Francophone Study** (1971) was a large-scale study which looked at 9, 12 and 15 year old French speakers in schools in Manitoba in Canada. Half the children did all their learning in classes where eighty percent of teaching was in French and twenty percent in English. The other half did their learning eighty percent of the time in English and twenty percent in French. At the end of the study, it was found that there was no difference between the two groups in their ability to read, write and speak in English. This is surprising indeed! Children who did only twenty percent of their learning in English were as good at English as children who did their learning in English eighty percent of the time. But the same could not be said for their home language. Children who did their learning eighty percent of the time in French were better at French than children who did their learning in French for twenty percent of their school time.

The study showed that even when children spend less time learning the school language, their progress does not suffer. But to develop the home language well, more school time needs to be given to learning it.

Interestingly, the study also found that the children who spent more time learning in their home language were also better at maths.

In 1972, the Alberta Provincial Government of Canada started the **Edmonton Ukrainian-English Bilingual Programme** in eight primary schools in Edmonton. People from Ukraine in Russia have settled in Canada for many years. Some families still use Ukrainian in the home but many families have lost their Ukrainian and can only speak English. Many families are now wanting their children to learn and use Ukrainian. In the programme, Ukrainian was used sixty percent of the regular school day throughout the primary school years. Only about fifteen percent of the children were fluent in Ukrainian when they started schooling. A study carried out with 6 and 9 year olds found that those using Ukrainian in the home were able to understand complicated *English* sentences better than children who came from English-Canadian homes or those children of Ukrainian origin who used English most of the time at home. Further studies of children who took part in this programme have shown that these children are not backward in English or other school subjects. Instead, by the time they have reached the age of 10 years, they are better at English reading comprehension skills than children not in the programme.

This study shows that learning one language helps in reading and understanding another language.

The Rock Point Navajo Study was started in 1971 and the first report written in 1976. The study was done in the USA with children who came from Navajo home, and whose home language was Navajo. (The Navajo, who were called Red Indians or American Indians at one time, are called Aboriginal or the First Nations people today.) Before the programme was started, Navajo speaking children were two years behind in their reading in English by the age of 12, compared to an average English speaking child in the USA. This was true even of Navajo speaking children who were receiving intensive teaching in English as a Second Language (ESL). The Rock Point programme started teaching Navajo to children when they were five years old and continued throughout primary school. Reading in English was not started until the children were eight years old and could read well in Navajo. By the time the Navajo children in the programme were 12, their English reading ability was *above* that of the average American 12 year old.

The study shows that building a foundation in the home language enables children to be better readers in the school language.

In the **Sodertalje Programme for Finnish Immigrant Children** in Sweden, the findings were very similar to those of the Rock Point Navajo Programme. Here the home language of the children was Finnish and the language of the school and the larger society was Swedish. Finnish children attending schools in Sweden, where they were only taught in Swedish, were found to be doing poorly in Swedish. Their spoken Finnish was also poor when compared to children in Finland. The Sodertalje programme used Finnish for teaching throughout the primary years. Swedish only became the main language in the school when the children were 9 years old. In this programme also, it was seen that by the time the children were 9 years old, they were better at Finnish than other Finnish speaking children not in the programme. Their Swedish was as good as other Swedish speaking children in the school.

So, teaching the home language to children helped them to be better at the language of the school even when they started learning the school language three years after starting school.

The **San Diego Spanish-English Language Immersion Programme** was started in 1975 in the San Diego city schools in California. In this programme, sixty percent of the children came from Spanish speaking homes and forty percent from English speaking homes. Teaching was done in Spanish right from the nursery years, with about 20 minutes of English every day, going up to 30 minutes in the first grade and 60 minutes in the second and third grades. The programme study showed that although the children lagged behind in both Spanish and English reading skills until they were nearly 12 years old, by the time they were 13, they performed above average in both Spanish and English. The performance of these children in maths was also above average.

This study also shows that using two languages regularly in the classroom helps children to learn better.

The **Carpinteria Spanish Language Preschool Programme** began in the Carpinteria School district in California, in 1979. Before the programme started, it was found that every year, the Spanish-speaking children coming into the nursery classes were not able to take part in all the learning activities that went on in the classroom. In school tests, given to all children entering the nursery, Spanish-speaking children scored lower marks *even when the tests were given in Spanish.* Before the programme started, Spanish-background children had been attending a bilingual preschool programme in which both Spanish and English were used but there was a strong emphasis on teaching these children English. The Spanish Language Preschool Programme used Spanish only to prepare Spanish-speaking children in such a way that when they joined school, their level of readiness was as good as the English-speaking children in the community. The programme also involved the parents closely and made them aware of their role as their child's first teacher.

The report on the programme says that:

> The development of language skills in Spanish was foremost in the planning and attention was given to every facet of the preschool day. Language was used constantly for conversing, learning new ideas, concepts and vocabulary, thinking creatively and problem solving to give children the opportunity to develop their language skills in Spanish to as high a degree as possible within the structure of the preschool day.

The surprising observation made in the programme was that although the preschool programme used Spanish only, in the *Bilingual Syntax Measure Test* (a test to measure a bilingual person's use of grammar in both the languages), these children performed better *both in English and in Spanish* than other Spanish-speaking children who were receiving additional English teaching. The writers of the report believe that the attention that was being given to Spanish in the programme enabled children to learn more of the English they were exposed to in the environment.

7

BOOKS ON BILINGUALISM

In the last twenty-five years, a large number of books have been written on the subject of bilingualism and language maintenance. Most of these books have been written for teachers and language scientists, so many parents and young people have not read them. Many of the ideas contained in these studies have been discussed in this book. The following pages give short summaries of some of these studies. As you can imagine, it is difficult to say in a few sentences what these books say in a hundred or more pages. However, my summaries show that there is plenty of support for bilingual education and a great deal of information on bilingual children and bilingual education. I shall try and give you the central message of each book. You may find some of particular interest and want to read them yourself.

A few hundred books have been written that explain the different sides of bilingualism and being bilingual. Some books focus on explaining how languages work (linguistics), others discuss the use of languages in society (sociolinguistics), while others explain the relationship between the mind and the use of two languages (psycholinguistics). Some books concentrate on the working of the brain and the use of two languages (neurolinguistics) and others are about bilingualism and education and about teaching the mother tongue. The books selected are the ones generally used in colleges and by teachers. Most of them explain the different sides of bilingualism — educational, social, psychological and neurological. They also explain what other language scientists have found and said about people using two languages. The first three books give very good summaries of what the language scientists have said about bilingualism in the last fifty years. Almost all the major studies of bilingualism and bilingual people are discussed in these three books.

Bilinguality and Bilingualism was first written in French by Josiane Hamers and Michel Blanc, and then published in English by Cambridge University Press in 1993.

The book deals thoroughly with a large number of different situations and different scientific findings about being bilingual. The book starts off by explaining how a person's ability to use two languages can be measured in different ways for different purposes. It then explores the relationship between intelligence and being bilingual; a bilingual person's mental development; bilingualism and society; different kinds of bilingual situations; the relationship between language and culture; how a bilingual person uses language. It discusses bilingual education; bilingualism and language development; and bilingualism and language interpretation.

In all, there are forty headings under which different aspects of bilingualism are discussed. This is a good scientific book that answers many of the questions about bilingualism that teachers might ask. The two authors, who have spent their lifetime studying bilingualism and bilingual children, are very clearly supportive of bilingual development and bilingual education.

Bilingualism, by Suzanne Romaine, was published by Basil Blackwell in 1989.

This too is scientific and thorough and is widely used by teachers and colleges. The book starts by describing the different kinds of bilingual situations and different ways of studying bilingualism. The second chapter describes the ways in which bilingual people use their languages in society. There is also a good explanation of the workings of the bilingual brain and the relationship between bilingualism and intelligence. Chapter 4 explains how bilingual people develop and use their two languages. Chapter 5 takes six bilingual children as examples to explain the different kinds of bilingual development that can take place.

The book goes on to describe what schools and education authorities can do about children's bilingualism. The last section discusses how bilingual people themselves view the use of two languages and how people using only one language view those who use two.

In conclusion, the author says that there are many kinds of bilingual people and bilingual situations but generally she supports healthy bilingual development in children and adults.

Life with Two Languages — An Introduction to Bilingualism, Francoise Grosjean, was published by Harvard University Press in 1982. Its 340 pages explain many things about bilingualism and answer many questions about using two languages.

The first part of the book discusses bilingualism in the world and shows how difficult it is to find a country in which only one language is used and how, in many parts of the world, people who use two or more languages arc respected for it. The second part of the book discusses countries like Belgium and Canada that have two official languages, and countries like India that have many official languages. The third part describes the bilingualism that exists in the United States — the two languages used by the Native Americans, deaf Americans, German Americans, French speaking Americans, and Americans who speak Spanish and English. It is interesting to see that there are so many people in America who speak and use English *and* another language.

The book then goes on to explain bilingualism in society. How people lose their mother tongue; how society can damage people's the opinion of themselves by being negative about their languages; how bilingual people mix their languages and how they come to be part of two cultures.

The next section discusses the bilingual child and explains how children may learn two languages together or one after another, how they mix languages and words, how they play with their languages. The section on a bilingual child's education explains how some countries try to make bilingual children lose their home language, and how in some countries the home language is taught only so that children may learn the language of the country and grow up losing their home language. The author supports the type of education that enables children to grow up using two languages and understanding two cultures.

The last two sections of the book explain the complicated workings of a bilingual person's brain and their use of language. It also explains that a person's brain does not get fixed on one or two languages at any age, so that the idea that it is only possible for a person to learn a new language before a certain age is untrue. It explains how a bilingual person's speech, sounds and grammar can develop in the two languages and how it is normal for languages and people to borrow words from each other.

Multilingualism and Mother-tongue Education is written by D.P. Pattanayak and published by Oxford University Press in 1981.

The introductory chapter is written by Ivan Illich, who has contributed a great deal to changing ideas about teaching young people. Illich takes us through history, using examples of Latin, Spanish and French to show how a language that belonged to everybody was changed by the ruling class into an instrument of power and control and how people who spoke a particular language or spoke a language in a particular way were given positions of power and authority. The chapter helps us to understand how certain languages were given more importance than the languages of ordinary people. It helps us to realise how we ourselves consider certain languages to be more pure than or superior to others.

The main part of the book contains nine chapters written by D.P. Pattanayak, derived from the various articles and papers that he gave at international conferences on education and language teaching. The chapter on mother-tongue and education of minority children would interest us most. The writer gives a report about the various studies of bilingualism. He makes a strong case that if we want people to have equality in education, political participation and individual growth, then it is of utmost importance that children are taught in the language they are most familiar with — the mother tongue, the home language or the first language. Children will then be able to learn the local, national and international languages which would lead to a fuller participation in society.

Bilingualism: Basic Principles, written by Hugo Baetens Beardsmore, is published by Multilingual Matters in 1982.

This book is widely used by teachers and student teachers. It starts by discussing what is meant by bilingualism and goes on to describe different kinds of bilingualism. It is surprising to see how many different ways there are of describing bilingualism and bilingual situations. The book helps us to see that the ability to speak two or more languages depends on what value society put on these languages; the age at which the child starts learning one or the other language; whether a language is taught in the school, or learnt in the home or neighbourhood; how much the school values that language; whether the parents value and encourage the one language or the other ; and so on. The book explains that there are many bilingual learning situations.

The second chapter describes how a child's two languages can influence each other and whether this situation is permanent or temporary. It also talks in detail about code switching.

The next chapter talks about the different ways of measuring a child's bilingualism. But more importantly, it discusses the studies that have tried to measure the relationship between bilingualism and mental ability. The chapter on theoretical considerations discusses the differences and similarities between development in one language and development in two or more languages. Special attention is given to the age at which the second language development takes place. Language scientists believe that certain things happen in the human brain after the teenage years which make learning another language quite different from growing up learning two languages at the same time from an early age.

The last chapter talks about the difficulties a child might face in learning two languages. Two cultures using two different languages can send confusing messages children and the book describes how they can overcome this difficulty. The second major difficulty is put upon the child by the school and the larger society. Do they value one language more than the other? Are they directly or indirectly telling children that one language is worth learning and the other a waste of time? Then the author goes on to discuss how and when a bilingual programme can be successful and in which conditions it can fail. There is also a very good criticism of the false ideas about bilingualism and language learning that many people and even some educators still hold in their minds.

Bilingualism or not? The Education of Minorities, by Tove Skutnabb-Kangas, was first published in Swedish in 1981. It was translated into English and published by Multilingual Matters in 1985.

This book focuses on the experience of bilingual education in Sweden, Finland, Denmark and Norway. It starts by explaining what a language is, what its uses are, and the different kinds of mother tongue learning situations there are. The book also gives very useful details of: What is meant by bilingualism? What are the different meanings of mother tongue? What are the different language learning situations? How can a child become bilingual with the help of the school and family? How is bilingualism measured? And what is the relationship between bilingualism and a child's mental and educational development?

Tove Skutnabb-Kangas is a strong supporter of bilingual education and bilingual language development. She believes strongly that in the early years, a child's education has to be in the home language. It is only after a firm foundation has been laid in the home language that the child can benefit from education in another language.

An important part of the book is the author's powerful case made against the poverty of education for children of immigrant parents in Western Europe. She lays the blame squarely on schools and educators for providing an inferior quality of education to these children. She makes a strong link between the political situation and how the new settlers in Western Europe are denied many of their basic rights. One of those basic rights is that children should be able to maintain and develop their mother tongue. The last part of the book explains how society uses mental and physical violence on parents and children to stop them from using and developing their home languages.

Bilingual Children: Guidance for the Family, by George Saunders, published by Multilingual Matters in 1983.

This book is very useful for parents in that it describes the experience of an English speaking family in Australia who brought up their children speaking English and German. The parents themselves did not grow up speaking German but learnt it as a foreign language later on their lives.

The book starts off by giving definitions of expressions used by language scientists. It goes on to explain what is meant by bilingualism and outlines the advantages of being bilingual. It tells how and why the family decided to encourage the use of German as well as English in the home. It gives details of what kinds of things the parents talked about and in which language: speaking, playing, story telling, reading, writing, talking with friends, in school and with each other. It also describes the development of the two languages in the children: the words they use, how they change from one language to another, and if the children get confused between the two languages. It also talks about what makes it difficult for children to develop their two languages, particularly their German. For example, how do the children feel about using their German? What about friends who only speak English? When the children speak in German, how are they made to feel by grownups around them who only speak English? And how do the schools and teachers feel about the children using German as well as English in the school?There is a good section on what the parents did to support their children's learning of German. This describes books, records, cassettes, radio and television, games, outings, shops and restaurants, language schools, visiting countries where German is spoken and receiving visitors from those countries, and writing letters in German.

The book is helpful to parents who would like to bring up their children using two languages, although it should be remembered that the two languages, English and German, are both important European and international languages, valued around the world. Parents who would like to encourage their children to keep an Asian, American or African language would face similar difficulties *and more*! Asian, American and African languages are generally less valued by the larger society, teachers and schools. The children themselves often grow up valuing their home languages less or not at all. Although it may be more difficult to maintain and encourage the use of such languages, the advantages of being bilingual are the same and the book is very helpful for ideas on the things parents can do at home to encourage children to learn and use another language.

Bilingualism and Special Education: Issues in Assessment and Pedagogy, by Jim Cummins, was published by Multilingual Matters in 1984.

This book is very important because it makes powerful arguments for bilingual education to teachers and educators. It discusses the experience of bilingual education in Canada and the United States. It talks about how the tests that a school uses to get information about bilingual children often give incorrect information because these tests arc written for children who speak one language only. In many cases, bilingual children are seen to be doing poorly in schools because many teachers regard bilingual children as children who have language problems and not as children who have additional or different language skills. Cummins explains how bilingual education can hclp children when they have built a foundation in the homc language first. He also explains in detail the difference between a bilingual child's ability to speak in the two languages in social situations and to use those languages in school and learning situations. This is followed by examples of some important long-term bilingual programmes (summaries of these programmes are given on pages 44-47 of this book).

The book explores *immersion programmes*, in which children, quite often from privileged homes, are sent to schools where teaching is in another language. The Canadian immersion programmes are world famous. In these programmes, children from English speaking homes spend time in schools where all learning takes place in French. Most children come out of the programme speaking good French and also reading and writing good French and English. However, this does not always happen when children from other language backgrounds are put into a totally English speaking school. In these cases, children first of all lose their home language and often their English does not develop satisfactorily. Cummins explains that this happens because the children are not immersed in the language but *sub*merged in it. He calls this kind of teaching *submersion*.

The later part of the book discusses the special difficulties that bilingual children can face in schools and how the schools can respond to these difficulties. It ends by stressing the importance of home language in a child's educational development and the important role that parents play in bilingual children's education.

Minority Education: From Shame to Struggle, edited by Tove Skutnabb-Kangas and Jim Cummins, was published by Multilingual Matters in 1988. Twenty-nine writers have each written a section. All have worked to develop bilingual education and anti-racist work with children.

As the title indicates, the main message of the book is that, after being made ashamed of their home languages through history, people should now fight to continue with the use and development of their languages in schools and the wider society.

The book starts with social and political explanations about why certain languages have been suppressed in the past and what the speakers of these languages have done about it. Examples are given from the USA, the Netherlands, The United Kingdom, Sweden and Canada.

The second part of the book describes some powerful experiences of people who, against all odds, have grown up continuing to use their two languages.

The third part gives examples of what people from different parts of the world have done to struggle for their educational rights. It is very encouraging to see that people from different parts of the world, whose histories and languages have been suppressed, denied or damaged, have succeeded in taking steps to improve their own situations and their children's educational opportunities. There are many success stories — some of them mentioned in the summaries of the various studies of bilingual programmes on pages 44 to 47 of this book.

The last section of the book looks at the whole world situation and how powerful languages like English dominate other languages of the world. The chapter on *Monolingual Myopia and the Petals of the Indian Lotus: Do more Languages Divide or Unite a Nation?* written by D.P. Pattanayak, inspired the design for the cover of this book. His chapter explains how in a person, the many languages, skills and cultural experiences are like the petals of the lotus flower and make a more complete human being. Similarly, whole societies or nations are richer and more complete when they have more skills, experiences and languages.

The last section of the book makes a strong statement that the use and maintenance of a person's home language is a basic human right. This basic right also gives power to individuals to progress in education and society.

Multilingualism in the British Isles, edited by Safder Alladina and Viv Edwards, was published by Longman in two volumes, in 1990.

Although this is not about studies of bilingual education, it contains very encouraging and useful information about how many languages in the United Kingdom and the Republic of Ireland have continued to be used in homes and taught to children. The chapters are written by people who grew up speaking and using the languages they write about.

The two volumes trace the history of the experiences of these languages. There is much to learn from the experiences of the various language groups about how they kept their language alive, how they resisted its suppression or loss, and how they taught the language to their children. Readers of the present book might like to read the chapter on their own home language in the book.

The first volume looks at the older mother tongues of the British Isles, like British Sign Language, Gaelic, Irish, Romani and Welsh. British Sign Language has been used by deaf people in Britain for centuries and is a language in its own right. Romani is the language of the Romani people who used to be called Gypsies and has been present in the British Isles for centuries. The book looks at languages with origins in East Europe: Hungarian, Lithuanian, Polish, Ukrainian and Yiddish; then from the Mediterranean area: Greek and Turkish from Cyprus, Italian, Portuguese, Spanish and Arabic of Morocco. Volume Two looks at the languages of West Africa, the Caribbean and Asia that are spoken in the British Isles. It describes the experiences of the languages of West Africa and the Caribbean creoles and then the languages of South Asia: Bengali, Gujerati, Hindi, Panjabi, Sinhala, Tamil and Urdu. The languages of East Asia — the Phillipines and Malaysia, the Chinese of Hong Kong and Vietnam and Japanese are discussed next, and then Farsi (Persian) and Hebrew from West Asia.

The central message of the two volumes is that there is a wealth of languages in the British Isles and English is not the only language spoken. One can imagine a similar wealth of languages that exists in countries such as the USA, Canada, Australia, South Africa, France and Germany.

8

CONCLUSION

The books described in the last section are only a sample from the hundreds that have been written on the subject. Other books and articles are less positive about bilingual development but the books I have mentioned answer the arguments against bilingualism. The purpose of the present book is really to put together arguments in support of bilingual development so that parents who would like their children to be bilingual can feel confident about supporting their bilingualism.

There are strong arguments from around the world for keeping and maintaining home languages. People are becoming more and more concerned today about saving animals, trees and forests. Is it not strange that people will give a lot to save whales, dolphins, tigers, rain forests and other endangered living things but not worry too much about languages being lost? Parents will do so much for their children to succeed but is it not strange that many parents will not worry much when their child loses a language? Instead of adding skills, such parents are helping children to lose a valuable skill.

To succeed in school and the larger society, it should not be necessary to give up one's home language. To be good at one language does not mean losing another. Parents should find ways of encouraging children to continue to use and develop their home languages — and this book has suggested some. In fact, people should find ways of not only keeping their own languages but also learning more languages. This way, we will be richer and more complete human beings.

9

DIRECTORY

This section is designed for parents or teachers to keep notes of the people and businesses that help to provide information and material for home language teaching.

Bookshops:

Computer programmes:

Language classes:

Teachers: